£1.00

my first number book

Marie Heinst

DORLING KINDERSLEY

London • New York • Stuttgart

DK

A Dorling Kindersley Book

Note to parents

My First Number Book is a practical introduction to basic number concepts for you and your child to share. The ideas presented in this book will help your child to develop an understanding of numbers at home and will provide a sound basis for the mathematics covered in the first years of school.

Each page offers topics for discussion, presented through fun number puzzles and interactive games. Take time working through the early pages that introduce the concepts of matching, sorting, and classifying. Ensure that your child can recognise and understand the number symbols 1-10, before moving on to the more advanced concepts of addition and subtraction. Wherever possible, supplement the puzzles on the page with number activities that arise in your child's daily routine and emphasize how numbers play an important role in everyday life.

Don't worry if, at first, your child has trouble in obtaining the correct answers, as mistakes are a valuable part of the learning process. It is much more important for children to explain their answers and to remain confident of their abilities. By working your way through this book together in a relaxed and supportive atmosphere, you will be helping your child to explore the world of numbers and gain a lasting enjoyment of mathematics.

Marie Heinst Mathematics consultant

Editor Andrea Pinnington
Art Editor Sharon Peters
Production Norina Bremner
Managing Editor Jane Yorke
Art Director Roger Priddy

Photography by Tim Ridley, Steve Shott

First published in Great Britain in 1992
by Dorling Kindersley Limited,
9 Henrietta Street, London WC2E 8PS

Reprinted 1992

A CIP catalogue record for this book is available from the British Library

ISBN 0-86318-786-2

Typeset by Setting Studio, Newcastle
Colour reproduction by Bright Arts, Hong Kong
Printed and bound in Italy by L.E.G.O.

Contents

Matching pairs

Two the same

All these things are found or used in **pairs**.
They are called pairs because they look the same.

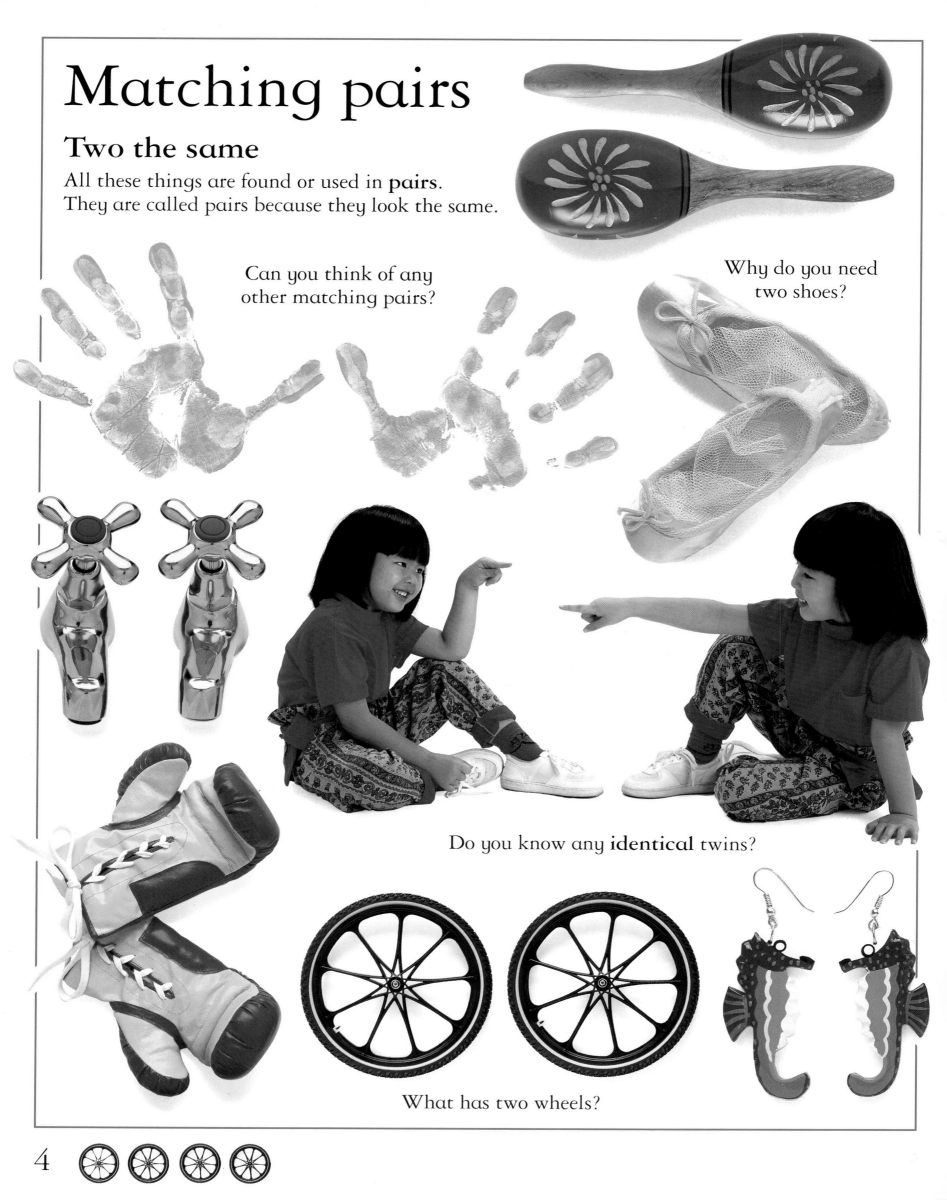

Can you think of any
other matching pairs?

Why do you need
two shoes?

Do you know any **identical** twins?

What has two wheels?

Partners

Can you imagine using a paintbrush without any paint, or a knife without a fork? These pairs are not the same, but they belong together as partners.

What other partners can you think of?

Pairs puzzle

How many pairs can you find? Which pairs look the same and which pairs are partners?

Can you find the one without a partner?

5

What goes where?

These five children have left some of their things at home.
Can you tell which objects belong to each child?

James   Helen   Daniel   Penny   Mark

Which outfit do you like best?

What is each of these children about to do?

What will Penny take with her to the seaside?

How many objects belong to James?

Who will use the snorkel and mask?

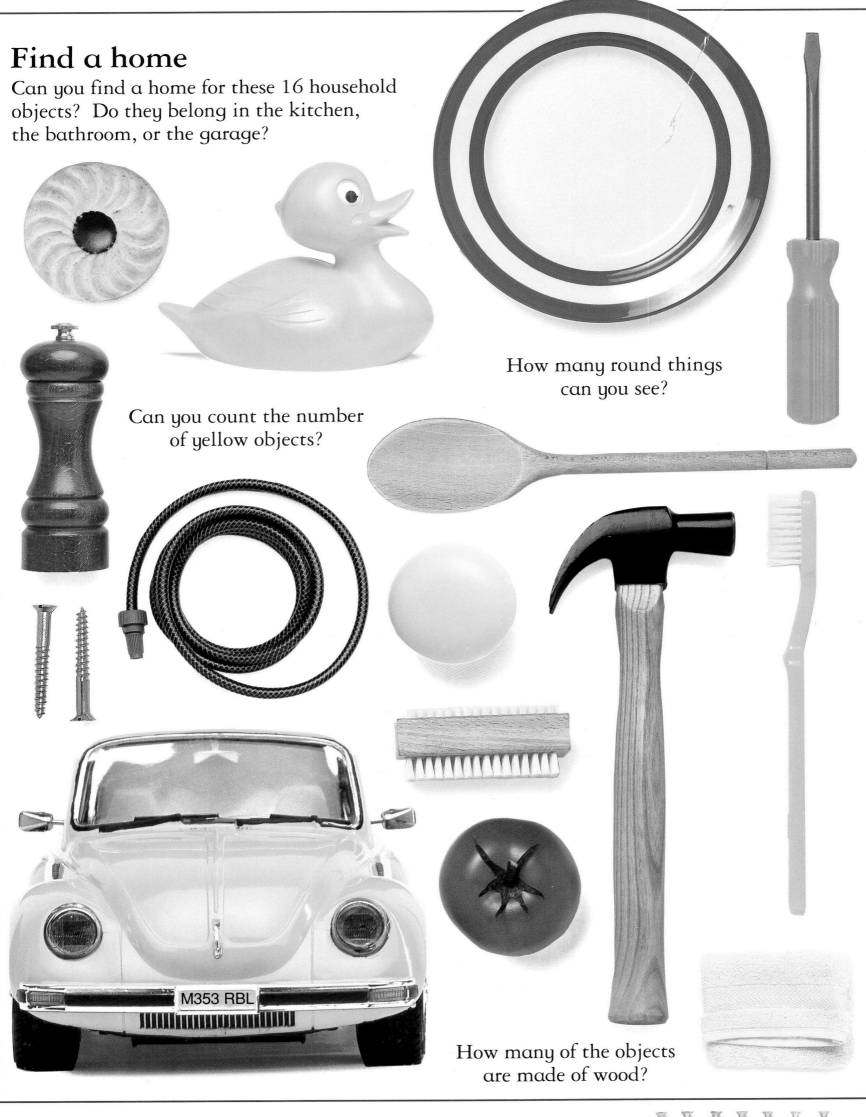

Find a home

Can you find a home for these 16 household objects? Do they belong in the kitchen, the bathroom, or the garage?

How many round things can you see?

Can you count the number of yellow objects?

How many of the objects are made of wood?

M353 RBL

Sorting sets

Here is a **set** of five cars. It is called a set because it is a **group** of things that belong together.

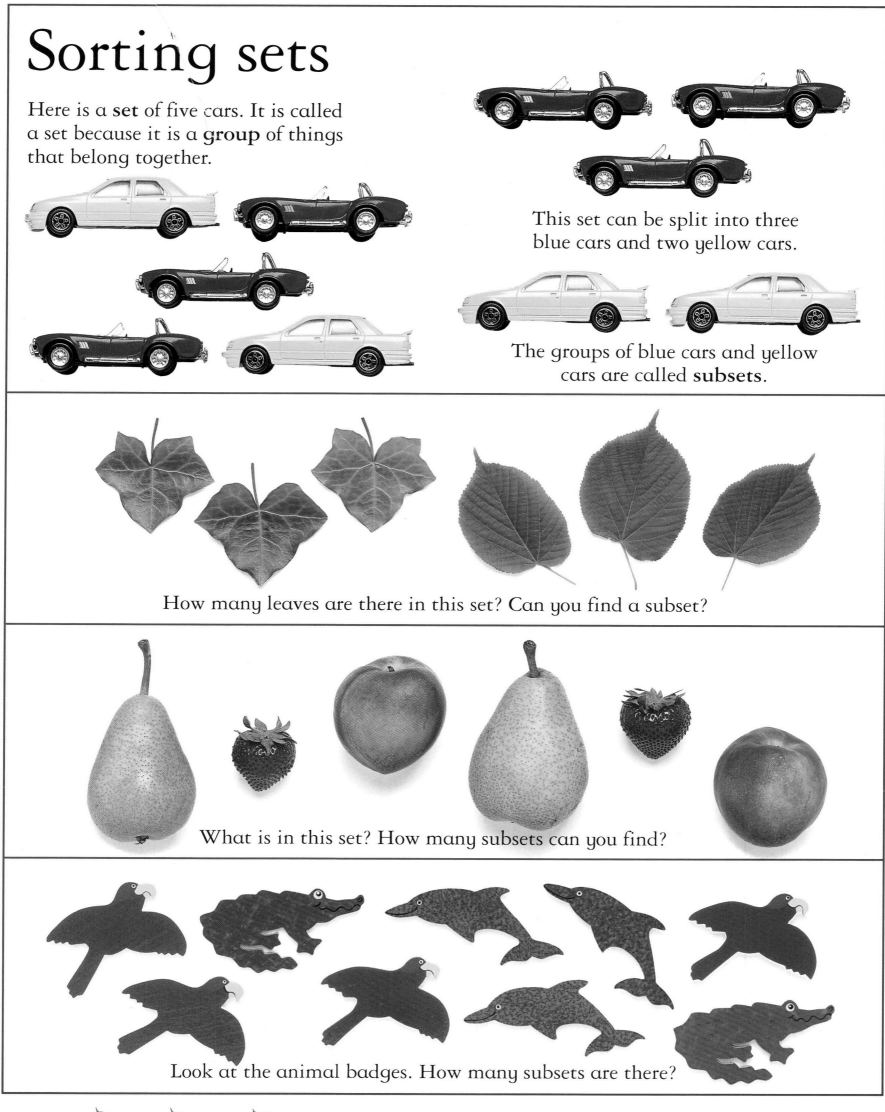

This set can be split into three blue cars and two yellow cars.

The groups of blue cars and yellow cars are called **subsets**.

How many leaves are there in this set? Can you find a subset?

What is in this set? How many subsets can you find?

Look at the animal badges. How many subsets are there?

8

Puppy puzzle

How many playful puppies can you see?
Count the sets of things that belong to them.

Are there enough collars
for all the puppies?

Will each puppy have a bowl of its own?

Can you spot
any subsets in
this group of
bouncy balls?

Can the puppies be
put into subsets?

Are there enough
bones for all the
hungry puppies?

Will any of the puppies be left out in the rain tonight?

Making patterns

A **pattern** is a design that repeats. Many patterns can be found in nature, such as the stripes on this snake.

How many red stripes can you count?

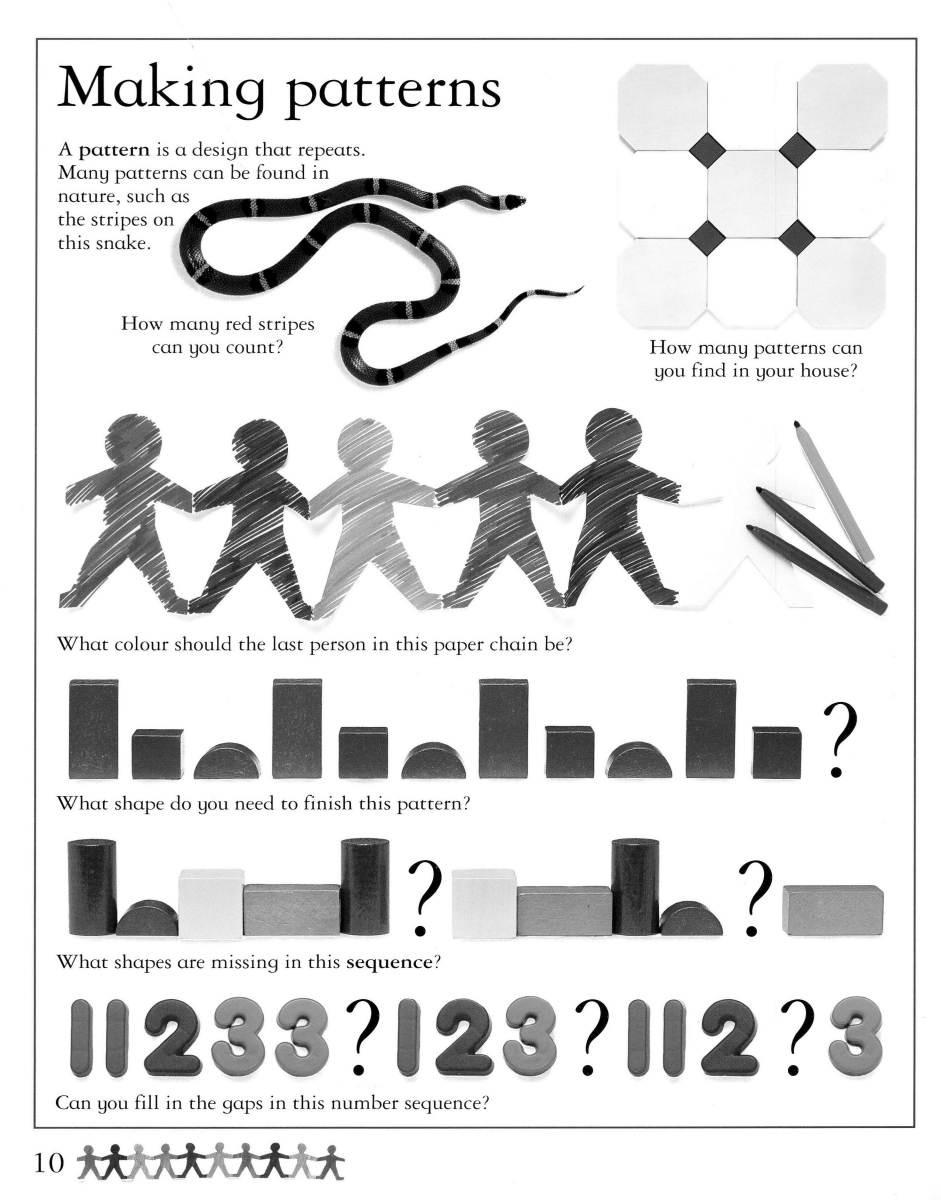

How many patterns can you find in your house?

What colour should the last person in this paper chain be?

What shape do you need to finish this pattern?

What shapes are missing in this **sequence**?

Can you fill in the gaps in this number sequence?

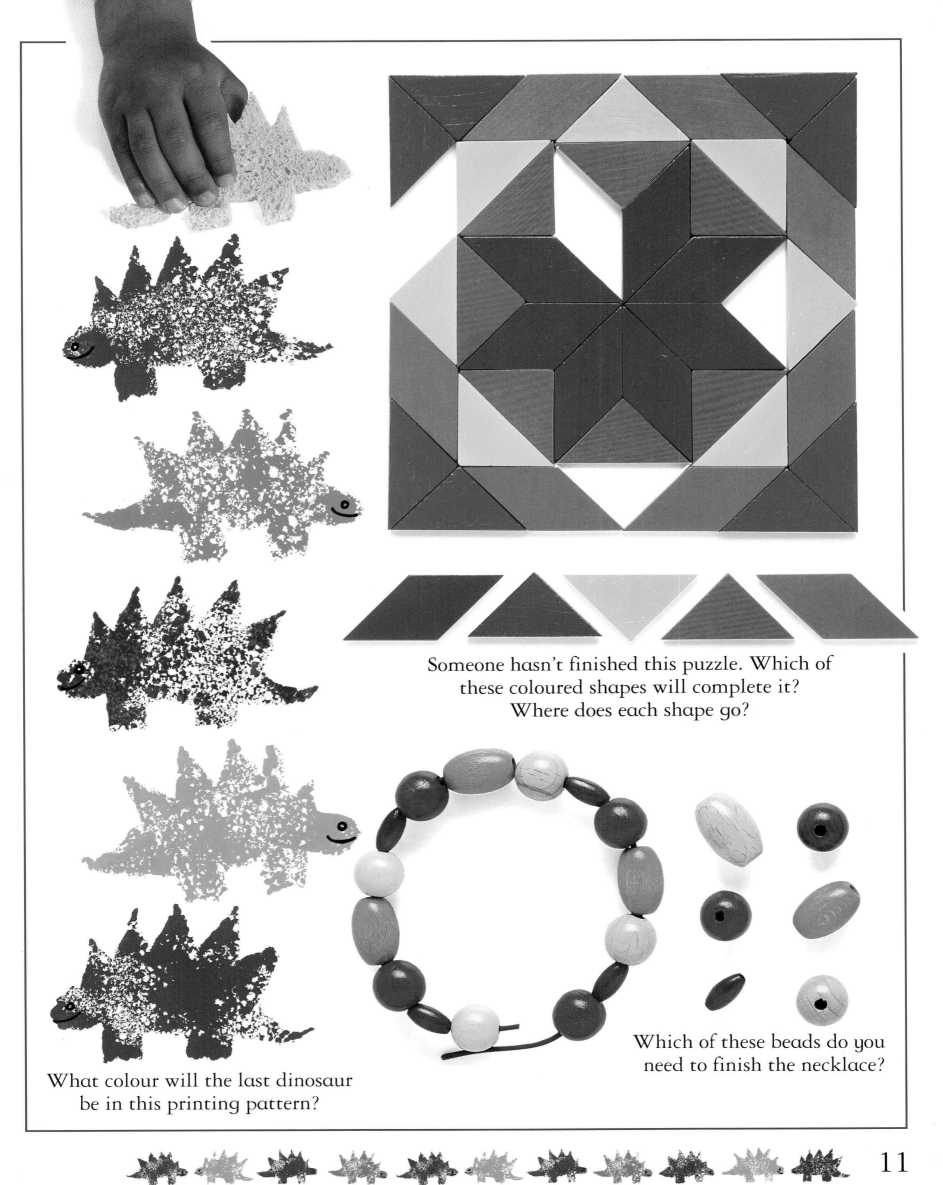

Someone hasn't finished this puzzle. Which of these coloured shapes will complete it? Where does each shape go?

What colour will the last dinosaur be in this printing pattern?

Which of these beads do you need to finish the necklace?

Are they the same?

Are there the same number of soldiers standing up as there are lying down? Count them and see.

How many candles can you count?

Are there the same number of candles on the birthday cake?

Are there the same number of loose beads as threaded beads?

Count the number of children in each group.

Are there more butterflies
fluttering in the air than
resting on the flower?

Are there more sweets lying loose
than in the packet?

How many bricks are
there in each shape?

Why do these shapes
look different?

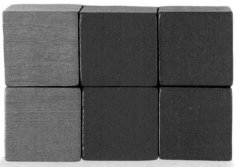

Does the number of children
stay the same however they
are arranged?

More or less?

How many pieces of fruit are there on each plate?

Which plate has more oranges than lemons on it?

How many animals can you count? Are there fewer chimpanzees than owls?

Are there the same number of round presents as square presents?

Which vase has the least number of yellow flowers in it?

Which vase of flowers do you like the most?

14

Teatime puzzle

Paul, Rebecca, Kim, George, Jack, and Amy are sitting down to have their tea. Whose plate would you like to have?

Paul

Count the slices of cake. Are there enough for everyone to have a piece?

Which plate has the fewest treats?

Rebecca

Amy

Kim

Does Kim have more gingerbread men than Jack?

Who has the least number of fruit tarts?

Jack

Does Amy have fewer fruit tarts than Paul?

George

How many napkins are there on the table?

15

In the right order

All these children are wearing shirts saying how old they are.

Who is the oldest?

Can you put these doors in the right order?

These cars are lined up for the race in the wrong order. How would you rearrange them?

Count each of these groups of pencils. Can you put them in the right order?

16

Number line

These ten children are now standing in order of age.
They are making a **number line**. You can use it to
help you to put things in the right order.

Which of these playing cards
is missing from the sequence?

Can you put these animals in order? Start with the one
with the fewest legs and end with the one with the most.

Can you help the
astronauts count
down to lift off?

First prize

Snail race

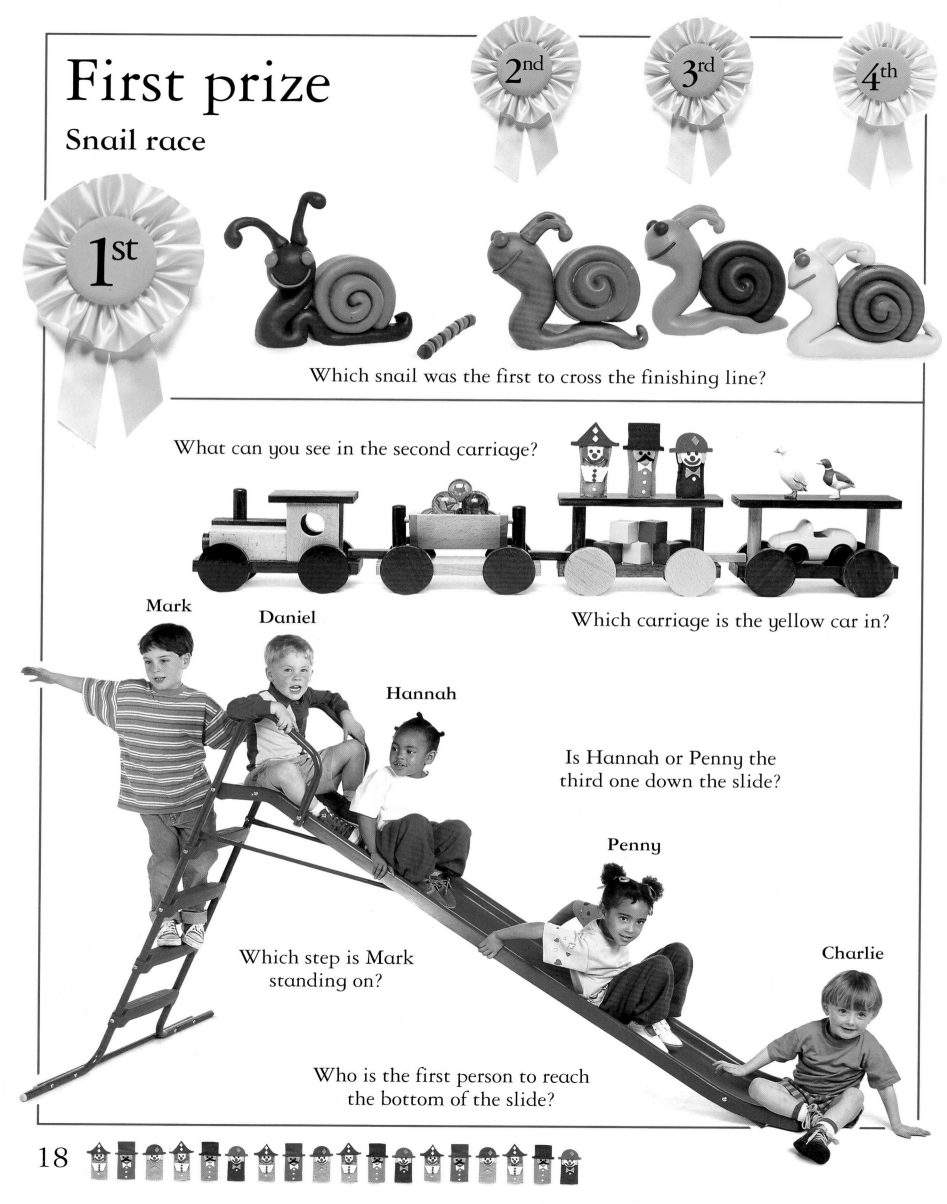

2nd 3rd 4th

1st

Which snail was the first to cross the finishing line?

What can you see in the second carriage?

Which carriage is the yellow car in?

Mark

Daniel

Hannah

Is Hannah or Penny the third one down the slide?

Penny

Which step is Mark standing on?

Charlie

Who is the first person to reach the bottom of the slide?

5th 6th 7th 8th 9th 10th

What colour is the seventh snail's shell?

Bookcase puzzle

This bookcase is packed full of toys. Can you help to sort them all out?

Where is the pot of paintbrushes?

How many teddy bears are there on the second shelf up?

Where is the big red alarm clock?

What toys can you see on the third shelf up?

Matching numbers

Count the number of garden bugs in each
group and match them to the numbers below.

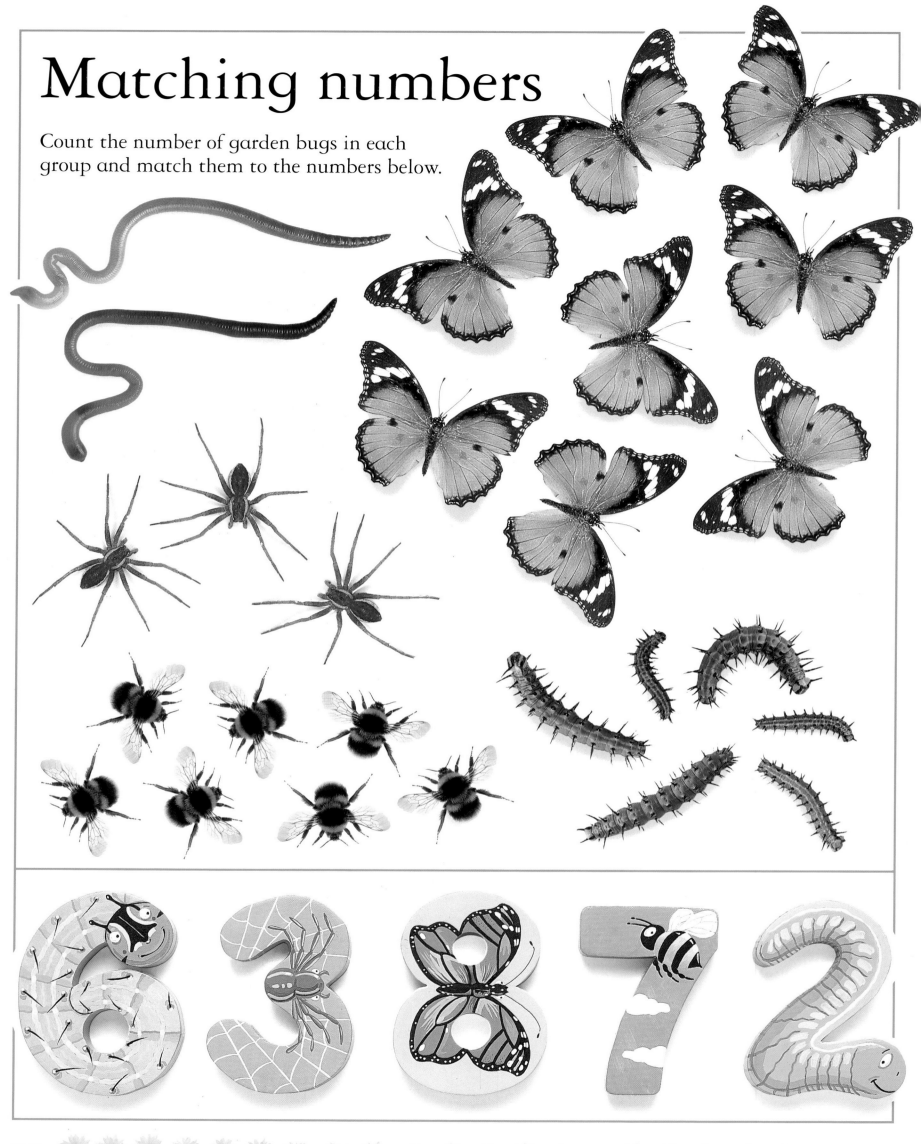

Garden puzzle

Try to match together all of the number sets between one and ten. When you find a matching set, cover the three blocks with coins or small pieces of paper. Look at this example to help you.

Number set:
Four garden spades belong with the number 4 and the block with four dots.

Spot the number

Numbers are all around us. Here are some examples of everyday objects that have numbers on them.

Can you find a bar code on this book?

The numbers on clocks and watches help us to tell the time. What time do you get up in the morning?

When you go shopping you will find the price of an item marked on a price tag or with a bar code.

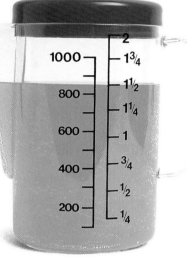

A measuring jug is used to measure different liquids.

What other things can you weigh?

Sunshine CORNFLAKES

375g

100 Jelly Beans

When would you need to use a **calculator**?

What do the numbers on these packets tell you?

A ruler is used for measuring things.

W.H. HAYDEN & CO. LTD.

22

Number trail

Look at the things on this page.
How do the numbers on them
help us in our daily lives?

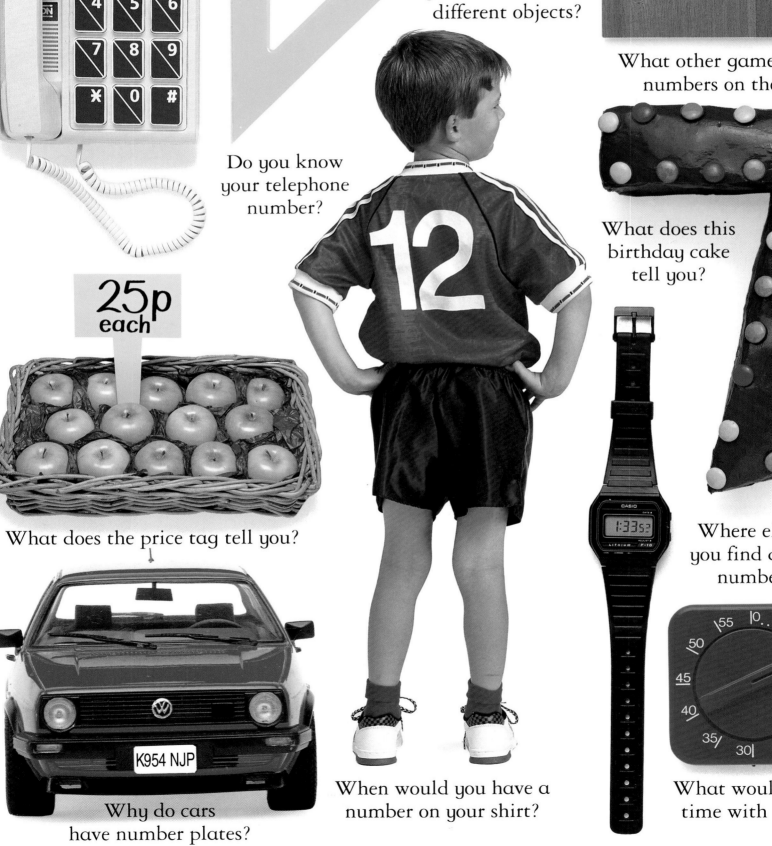

What else could
you use to measure
different objects?

What other games have
numbers on them?

Do you know
your telephone
number?

What does this
birthday cake
tell you?

25p each

What does the price tag tell you?

Where else do
you find digital
numbers?

Why do cars
have number plates?

When would you have a
number on your shirt?

What would you
time with this?

Hopping frog game

Who will be the first to hop through this magic garden? Each player will need one counter or small object. Put the counters on START and take turns throwing the dice. Move forward the number of places shown on the dice, but beware of the obstacles on your way!

dice

counters

START

Slip on moss. Hop back 4 stones.

Catch fly. Leap forward 3 stones.

Meet big toad. Miss 1 go.

34 35 36 37 38

Stop to talk
to friends.
Hop back
2 stones.

33

32

40

31

41

Swim through
pond.
Leap forward
5 stones.

42

43

FINISH

29

44

28

Kissed by
princess.
Hop back
to START.

49

27

48

46 47

How many altogether?

Number line

You can use a number line to help you to **add** up. To add 5 orange and 5 raspberry ice lollies, put your finger on the number 5 and count forward 5 places. How many ice lollies are there altogether?

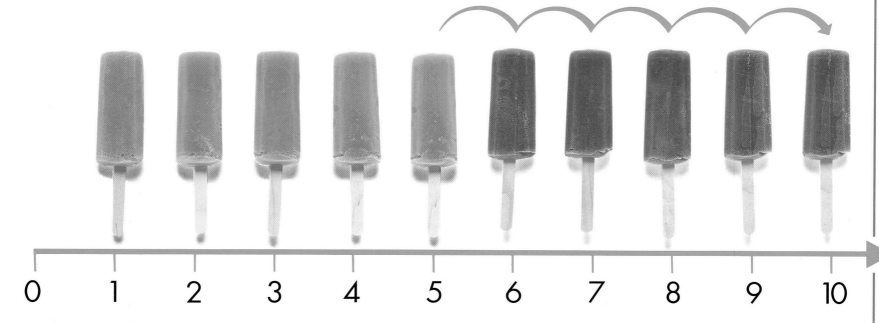

$$0 \quad 1 \quad 2 \quad 3 \quad 4 \quad 5 \quad 6 \quad 7 \quad 8 \quad 9 \quad 10$$

Use this number line to help you to solve the seaside puzzles below.

2 sandcastles on the beach.

1 more sandcastle is built.

How many sandcastles are there now?

4 sailing boats.

1 more boat comes sailing by.

How many sailing boats are there altogether?

7 fish swimming in a shoal are joined by 3 more fish.
How many fish are there altogether?

Treasures on the beach

Help this pirate and sailor to count up the
treasures they have found on the beach.

Count the number of pebbles
in each pile of treasure.

Who has the most
gold coins? How many
gold coins are there
altogether?

How many
shells are there
altogether?

How many starfish are there altogether?

How many necklaces can you count?

Adding up

Can you add these owls together?

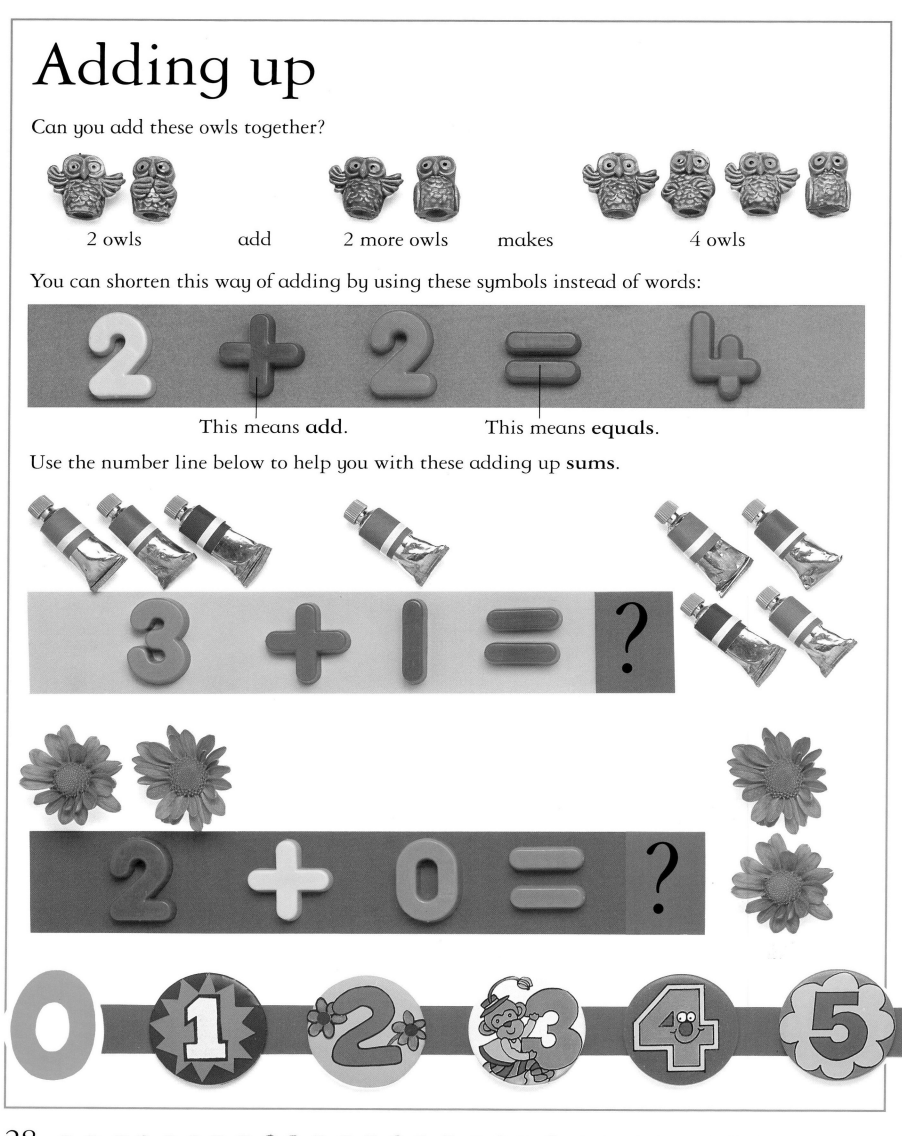

2 owls   add   2 more owls   makes   4 owls

You can shorten this way of adding by using these symbols instead of words:

2 + 2 = 4

This means **add**.   This means **equals**.

Use the number line below to help you with these adding up **sums**.

3 + 1 = ?

2 + 0 = ?

0   1   2   3   4   5

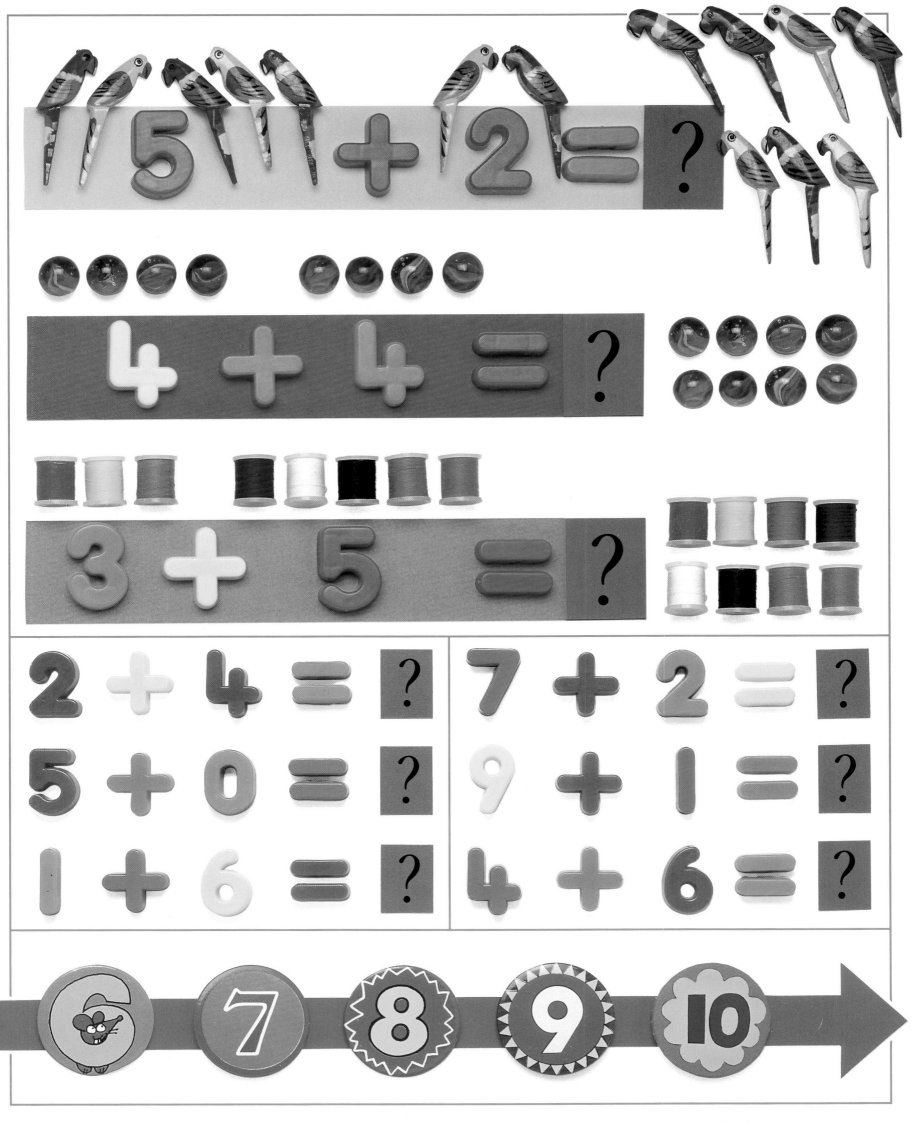

$5 + 2 = ?$

$4 + 4 = ?$

$3 + 5 = ?$

$2 + 4 = ?$

$5 + 0 = ?$

$1 + 6 = ?$

$7 + 2 = ?$

$9 + 1 = ?$

$4 + 6 = ?$

6 7 8 9 10

How many are left?

Number line

You can also use a number line to help you to **take away**. To take 4 glasses away from 10, put your finger on the number 10 and count back 4 places. How many glasses will be left?

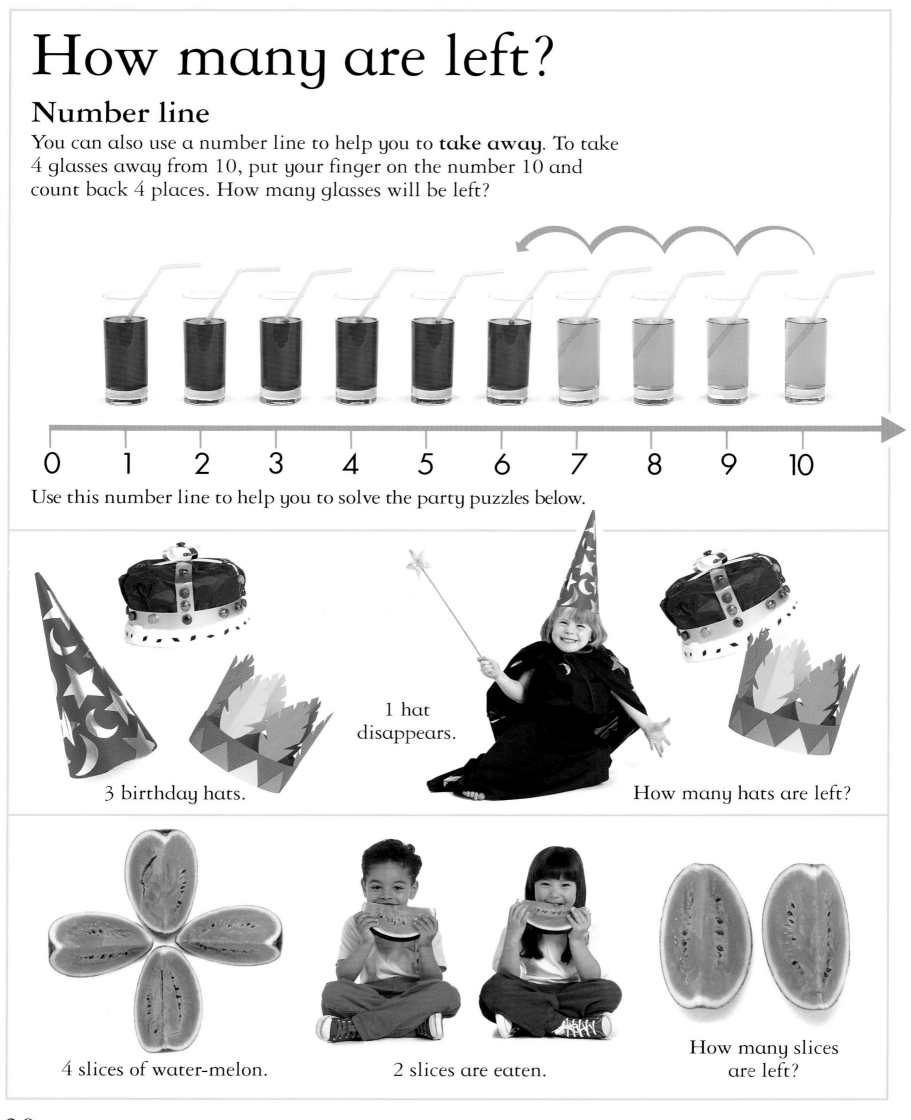

Use this number line to help you to solve the party puzzles below.

3 birthday hats.

1 hat disappears.

How many hats are left?

4 slices of water-melon.

2 slices are eaten.

How many slices are left?

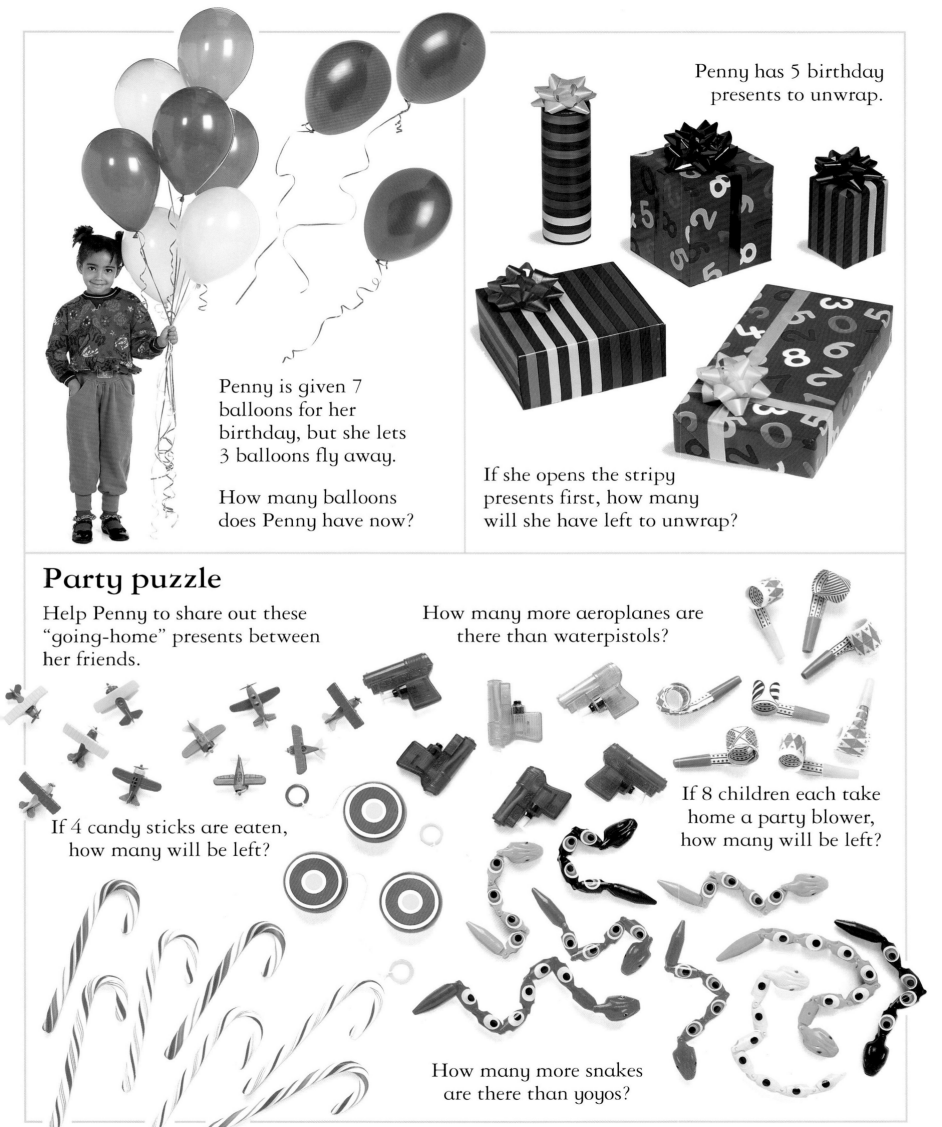

Penny has 5 birthday presents to unwrap.

Penny is given 7 balloons for her birthday, but she lets 3 balloons fly away.

How many balloons does Penny have now?

If she opens the stripy presents first, how many will she have left to unwrap?

Party puzzle

Help Penny to share out these "going-home" presents between her friends.

How many more aeroplanes are there than waterpistols?

If 4 candy sticks are eaten, how many will be left?

If 8 children each take home a party blower, how many will be left?

How many more snakes are there than yoyos?

Taking away

Can you take away these bears?

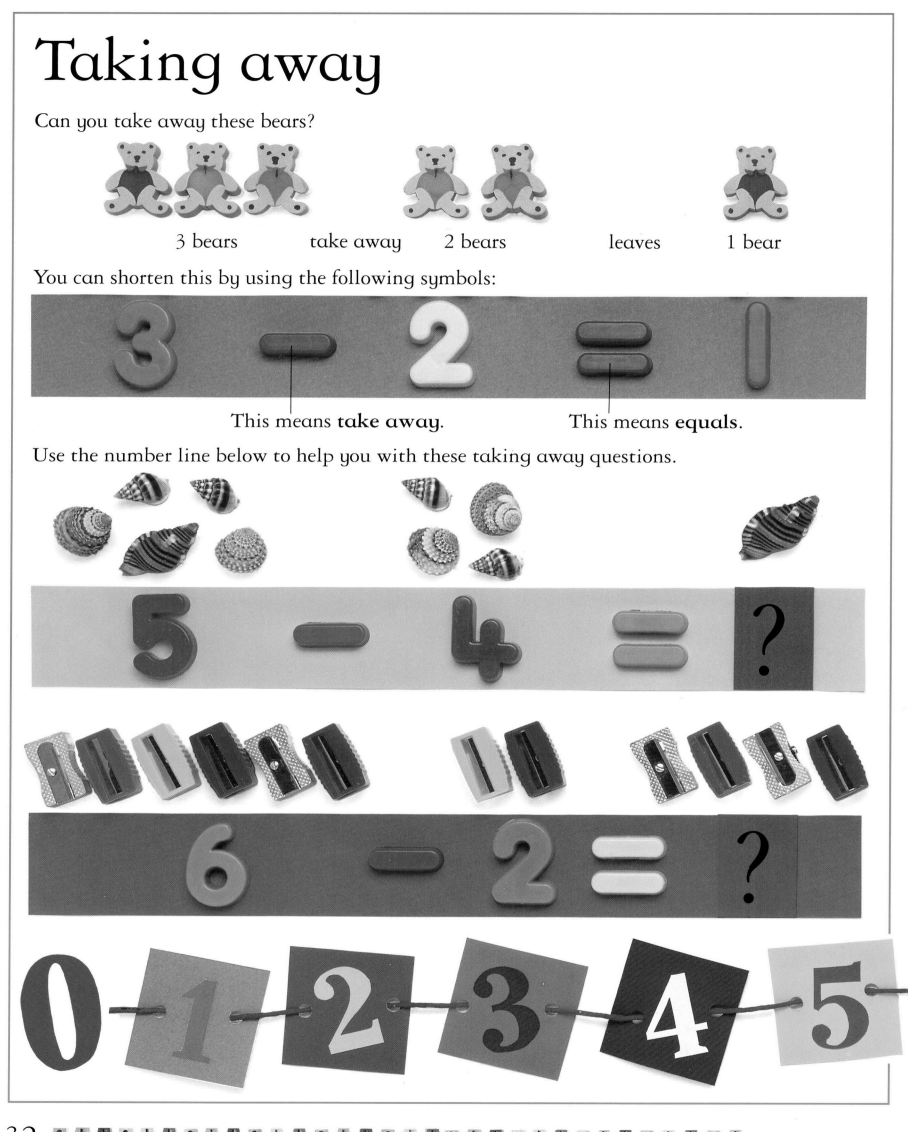

3 bears   take away   2 bears   leaves   1 bear

You can shorten this by using the following symbols:

3 — 2 = |

This means **take away**.   This means **equals**.

Use the number line below to help you with these taking away questions.

5 − 4 = ?

6 − 2 = ?

0 1 2 3 4 5

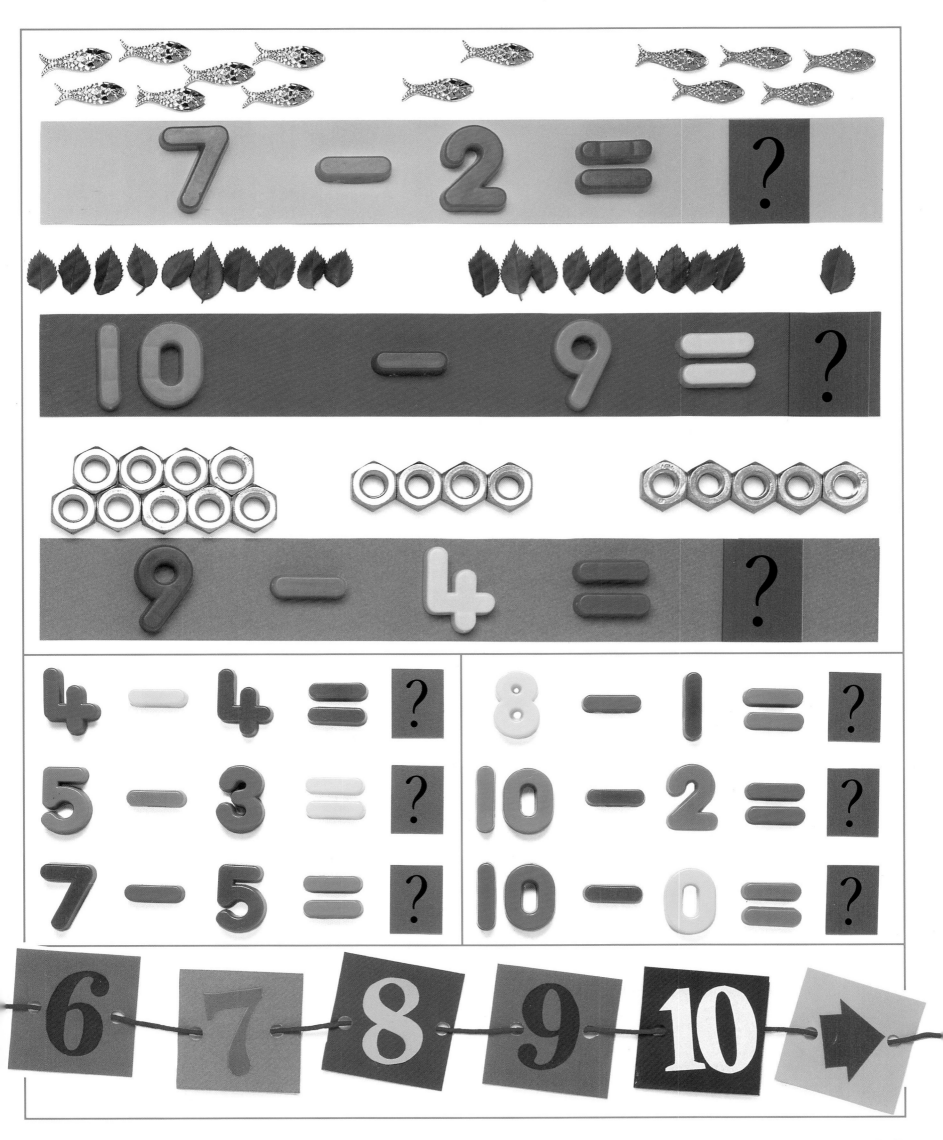

7 − 2 = ?

10 − 9 = ?

9 − 4 = ?

4 − 4 = ?

5 − 3 = ?

7 − 5 = ?

8 − 1 = ?

10 − 2 = ?

10 − 0 = ?

6 7 8 9 10 →

Different sizes

Which is the smallest wooden doll?

Wide and narrow

What colour is the widest ribbon?

Thick and thin

Which of these musicians is taller?
Who has the bigger musical instrument?

Here are two
coloured felt pens.
Which one is thick
and which one is thin?

Long and short

Is the ruler longer or shorter than the tape measure?

Big and small

Are you taller or shorter than your friends?

Who is sitting in the bigger space in the climbing frame?

Spot the difference

Can you spot the different sizes in these groups of objects?

What colour is the widest belt?

Is the yellow belt the narrowest?

Can you point to the thickest and the thinnest slice of bread?

What colour is the tallest bottle?

Are any of these bottles the same height?

What can you measure?

We often need to **measure** the things around us.

You can use different parts of your body to measure the objects around your home or school.

a reach

a handspan

a cubit

a pace

a footstep

How many footsteps?

Amy, Andrew, and Simon are busy measuring. How many things can you find around you to measure in different ways?

How many cubits long is the fish tank?

Can Simon reach across this playhouse?

Amy and Andrew are measuring this carpet. What sort of measurements are they using? Will they both take the same number of steps to cross the carpet?

Everyday measurements

You can use almost anything to measure different objects.

How many fingers are needed to measure two pencils?

How tall are you?

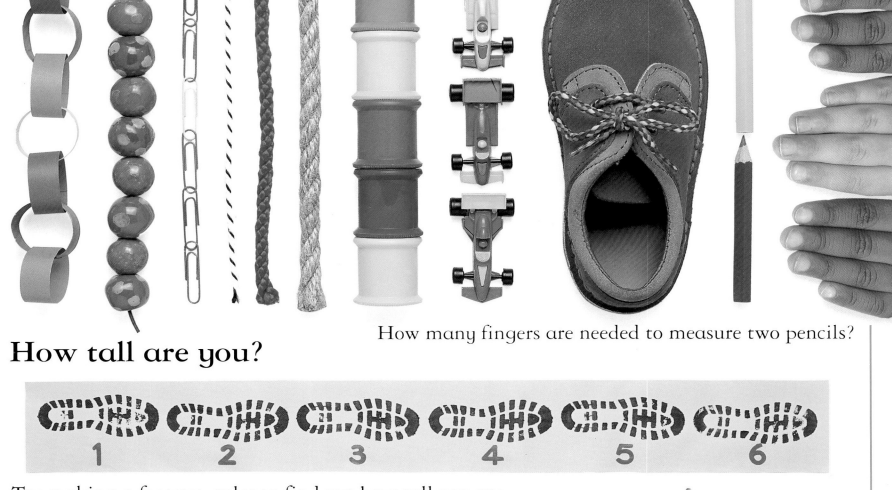

Try making a footstep ruler to find out how tall you are.

Is Amy shorter than Simon?

How many footsteps does Simon measure?

Is Andrew the same height as Simon?

Is the blue rope longer or shorter than the hatstand?

Heavy or light?

Matthew and Laura have packed their suitcases ready to go on holiday.

Which suitcase do you think is heavier?

When would a very big suitcase weigh less than a small one?

Laura is trying to lift her big suitcase. Why is she having trouble with it?

All these piles look about the same size. Which pile do you think is the heaviest?

Matthew and Fiona are **balancing** on the seesaw. What can you tell about their weight?

What would happen if Fiona was lighter than Matthew?

Fiona

Matthew

Guess the weight

To guess the weight of different objects, try feeling them in your hands.

Laura is holding pebbles in one hand and feathers in the other. Which pile is heavier?

Look at these weighing scales. Did you guess correctly?

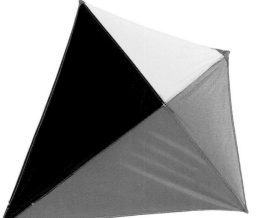

Are these weights lighter than the kite?

Are the wet towels heavier than the dry towels? Why?

Do you think three forks are lighter than three spoons?

Do the kitten and the truck weigh the same?

Is one pineapple lighter than lots of crisps?

What shape is it?

Flat shapes

How many of these shapes do you know?

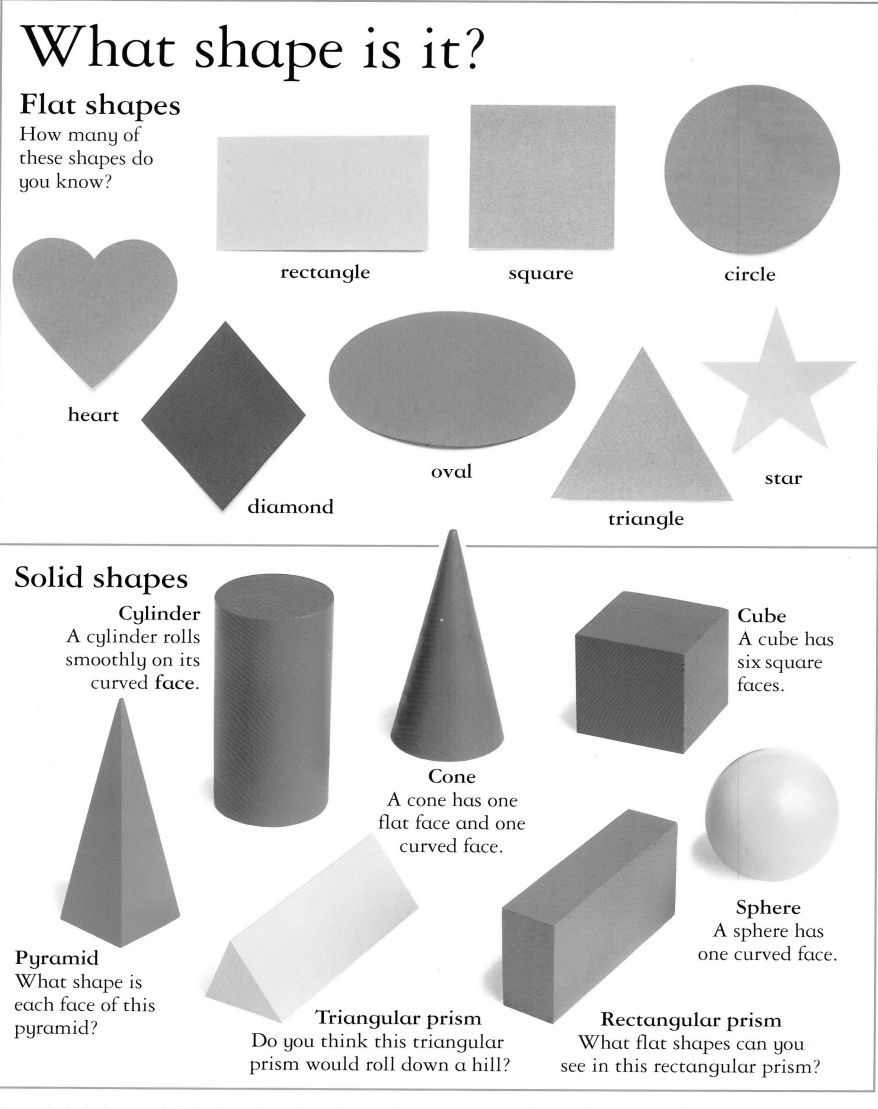

rectangle

square

circle

heart

diamond

oval

triangle

star

Solid shapes

Cylinder
A cylinder rolls smoothly on its curved **face**.

Cone
A cone has one flat face and one curved face.

Cube
A cube has six square faces.

Sphere
A sphere has one curved face.

Pyramid
What shape is each face of this pyramid?

Triangular prism
Do you think this triangular prism would roll down a hill?

Rectangular prism
What flat shapes can you see in this rectangular prism?

Shapes puzzle

Here is a collection of everyday objects found around the home.

Can you name all the shapes that appear in this puzzle?

Can you count all the spheres?

How many yellow triangles can you find?

How many squares are there?

How many hearts are there?

Which of these objects can you roll?

How long does it take?

Some things take a long time to do, and other things can be done very quickly.

How long do you think it takes to grow a seed: hours, days, or weeks?

Does it take minutes, hours, or days to bake some cakes?

How long does it take to blow up a balloon?

Fast or slow?

Does it take you a long time or a short time to do these things: get dressed, do a jigsaw, draw a picture?

Measuring time

Here are some things that we use to measure time. Have you ever used any of them?

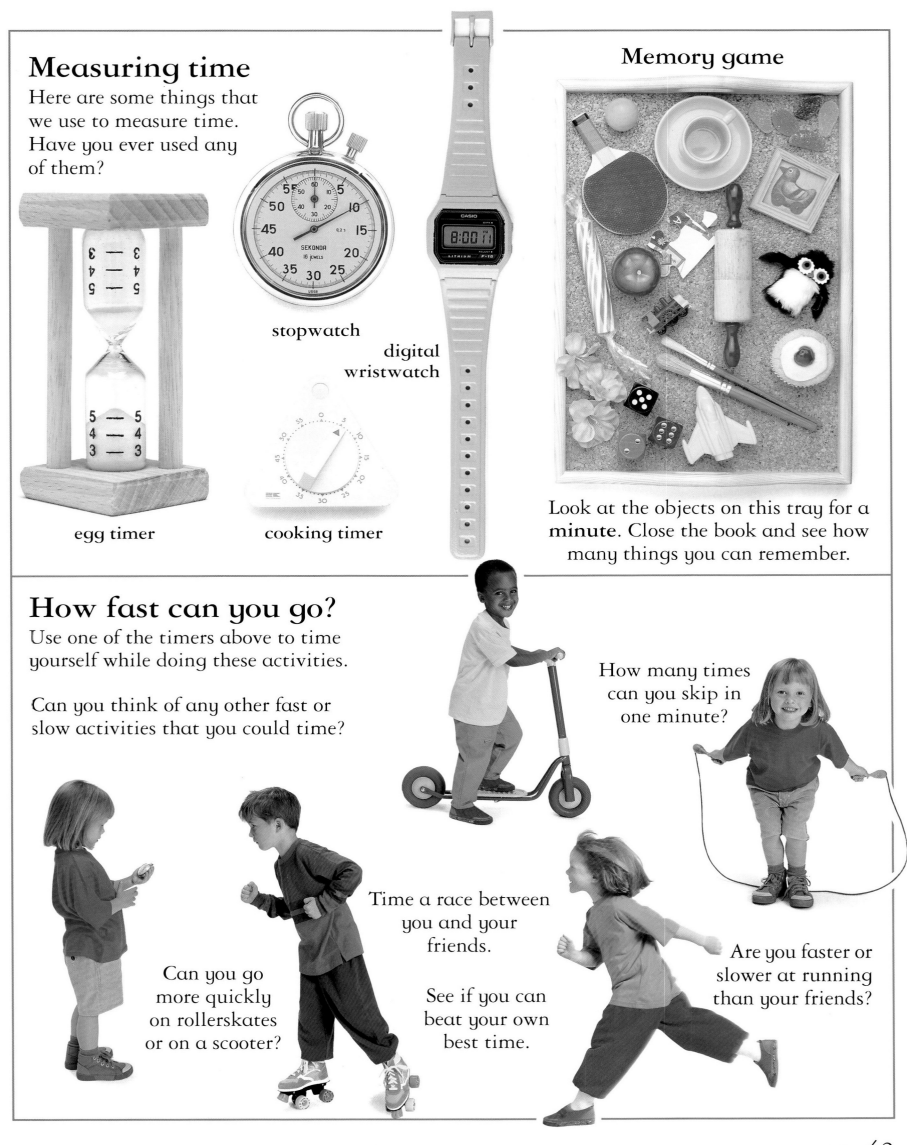

egg timer

stopwatch

cooking timer

digital wristwatch

Memory game

Look at the objects on this tray for a **minute**. Close the book and see how many things you can remember.

How fast can you go?

Use one of the timers above to time yourself while doing these activities.

Can you think of any other fast or slow activities that you could time?

Can you go more quickly on rollerskates or on a scooter?

Time a race between you and your friends.

See if you can beat your own best time.

How many times can you skip in one minute?

Are you faster or slower at running than your friends?

Counting up

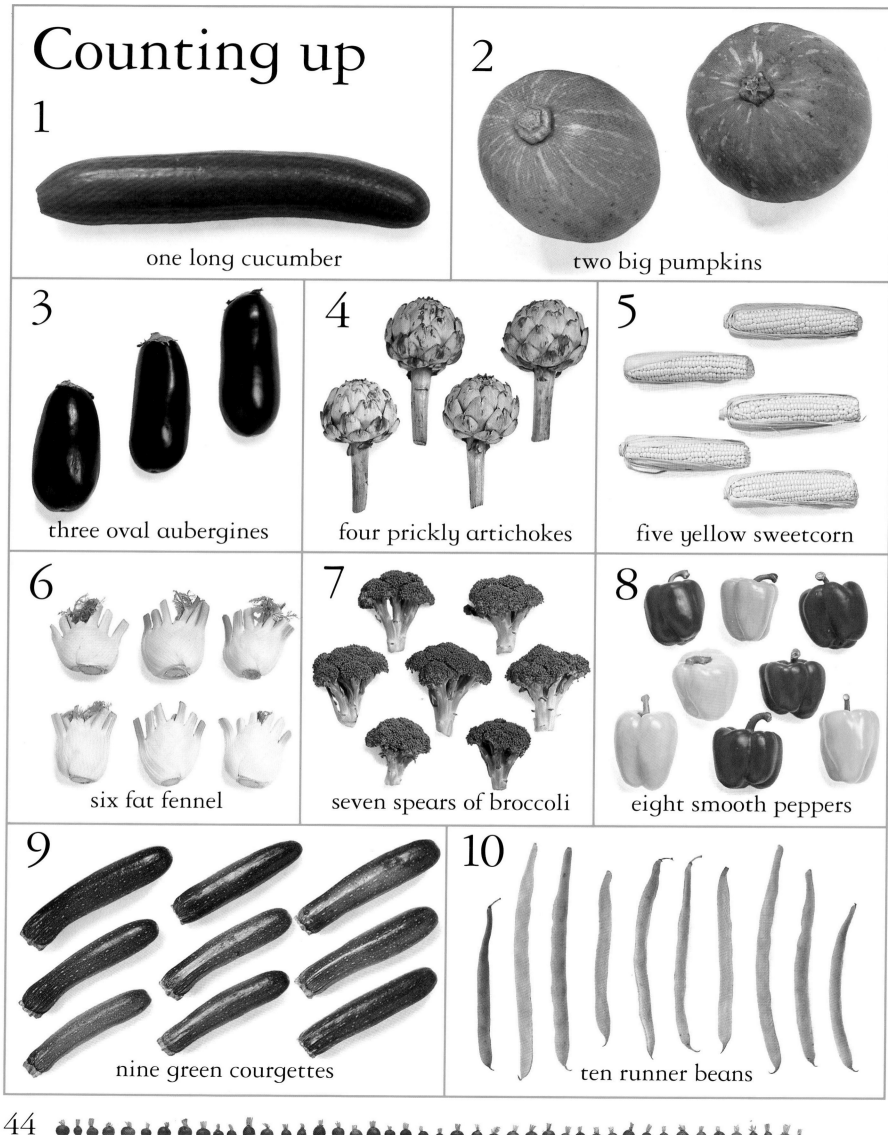

1

one long cucumber

2

two big pumpkins

3

three oval aubergines

4

four prickly artichokes

5

five yellow sweetcorn

6

six fat fennel

7

seven spears of broccoli

8

eight smooth peppers

9

nine green courgettes

10

ten runner beans

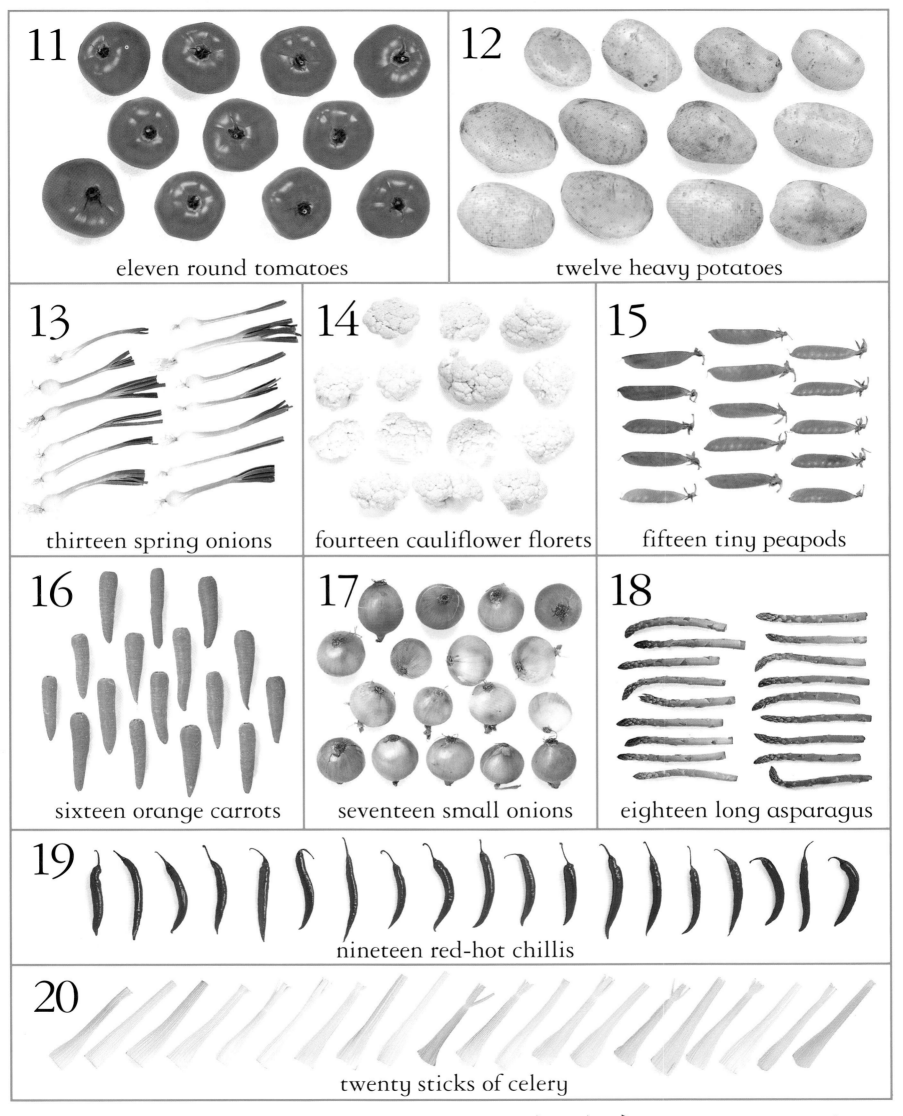

11 eleven round tomatoes

12 twelve heavy potatoes

13 thirteen spring onions

14 fourteen cauliflower florets

15 fifteen tiny peapods

16 sixteen orange carrots

17 seventeen small onions

18 eighteen long asparagus

19 nineteen red-hot chillis

20 twenty sticks of celery

Big numbers

20   twenty clothes pegs

50   fifty stars

100   one hundred buttons

500   five hundred beads

1,000   one thousand sweets

Number words

add (+)	To add is to find the sum of two or more numbers.	page 26
balance	To balance is to have the same weight on each side.	page 38
calculator	A calculator is an instrument to help you work out number problems.	page 22
equals (=)	An equals sign is used where two or more numbers have the same total value as another number.	page 28
face	A face is one surface of a solid shape.	page 40
flat shapes	Flat shapes are shapes that have height and width.	page 40
group	A group is any number of things that are gathered together.	page 8
identical	Two or more objects that are exactly the same are said to be identical.	page 4
mathematics	Mathematics is the study of number, measurement, shape, and space.	
measure	To measure is to work out the size, weight, or volume of something or somebody.	page 36
minute	A minute is a unit of time. There are 60 minutes in one hour.	page 43
number	A number is the name for a counting symbol.	
number line	A number line is a line of ordered numbers used for counting.	page 17
pair	A pair is a set of two things that match or belong together.	page 4
pattern	A pattern is a design that repeats.	page 10
sequence	A sequence is when one thing follows another in a fixed or regular order.	page 10
set	A set is a group of things that belong together.	page 8
solid shapes	Solid shapes are shapes that have height, width, and depth.	page 40
subset	A subset is a smaller group of things that belong together within a larger set.	page 8
sum	The sum is the total when two or more numbers are added together.	page 28
take away (-)	To take away is to find the difference between two numbers by deducting one from the other.	page 30

Acknowledgements

Additional Photography: Peter Chadwick, Steve Gorton

Many thanks to Penny Britchfield, Mandy Earey, Nicki Simmonds, and Mark Richards, without whose design help this book would not have been possible. Thanks also to Angela Wilkes for her help in conceiving the book; Hilary Foster and Fiona Lillywhite our home economists; Tom Messenger, Steve Cummisky, and Sarah Lindsay for their help in producing the book.

Dorling Kindersley would like to give special thanks to the many models: Andrew Abello, Jodie Alexis, Hannah Capleton, Bianca Clark, Reiss Claxton, Gemmel Cole, Laura-Lee Dockrill, Peter Dokic, Natalie Ellis, Lewis Greening, Karla Harris, Albert Hayden, Matjaz Kecek, Shelby Johnson, Lateef Joseph, Corinne Laidlaw, Tony Locke, Charlie McCarthy, Fiona McKenzie, Paul Miller, Chancelle Nardelli, Kim Ng, Jack Richards, Daniel Sach, Alexander Smith, Joe Tulino, Ahmani Vidal-Simon.